A

# REPLY

TO THE

# STRICTURES OF LORD MAHON AND OTHERS,

ON

THE MODE OF EDITING

THE

# WRITINGS OF WASHINGTON.

---

By JARED SPARKS.

---

CAMBRIDGE:
JOHN BARTLETT,
Bookseller to the University.
1852.

CAMBRIDGE:
METCALF AND COMPANY,
PRINTERS TO THE UNIVERSITY.

# NOTICE.

Strictures on the method pursued by the editor of "Washington's Writings," in preparing that work for the press, first appeared in the New York Evening Post. Hence the following remarks, intended as a reply, were directed in the form of letters to the editors of that Journal, in which they were originally published.

# REPLY.

---

## LETTER I.

ON THE GENERAL CHARGE OF TAKING AN UNWARRANTABLE LIBERTY IN ALTERING THE TEXT OF WASHINGTON'S LETTERS.

Some time ago there appeared in your paper several communications containing comments on two or three letters in "Washington's Writings," apparently designed to show the incompetency of the editor of that work for the execution of his task, and to place his fidelity in a questionable light. Ill health at the time prevented me from taking such notice of those comments, as their character and tendency might seem to require. From a recent article in the Evening Post, I learn that Lord Mahon, in a work lately published, has repeated them, and added strictures of his own. I am constrained, therefore, to ask the attention of your readers to a few remarks touching this matter.

The charge made by the writer in the Evening Post, and adopted by Lord Mahon, is, that the editor of "Washington's Writings," in preparing the manuscripts for the press, has taken an unwarrantable liberty with the text, altering, omitting, and adding, as might suit his caprice, and that, for the purpose of embellishment and of conforming the work to his own standard of taste, he has "tampered with the truth of history."

I deny that any part of this charge is true, in any sense which can authorize the censures bestowed by these writers, or raise a suspicion of the editor's fidelity and fairness. It would certainly be strange, if an editor should undertake to prepare for the press a collection of manuscript letters, many of them hastily written, without a thought that they would ever be published, and should not at the same time regard it as a solemn duty to correct obvious slips of the pen, occasional inaccuracies of expression, and manifest faults of grammar, which the writer himself, if he could have revised his own manuscripts, would never for a moment have allowed to appear in print.

This is all I have done in the way of altering or correcting Washington's letters. The alterations are strictly verbal or grammatical; nor am I conscious that, in this process, an historical fact, the expression of an opinion, or the meaning of a sentence, has, on any occasion, been perverted or modified. I can confidently affirm that the editorial corrections were never designed to have such a tendency, and, if such should anywhere appear to exist, it must be accidental and of little significance. What possible motive could there be for assuming such a license? Washington's character certainly did not require to be protected by so unworthy an artifice; and least of all could the editor derive from it either fame, profit, or any other conceivable advantage.

These verbal alterations chiefly occur in the private letters, which were written in haste and not intended by the author for publication; and they make but a comparatively small portion of the work. In his official correspondence, and papers prepared for the public eye, no man was more precise and careful than Washington as to the selection of his words and the construction of his language. His private and confidential letters, like those of other men, were often negligently written in regard to these particulars. This class of letters, I thought it the duty of an editor, as an act of justice to the memory of the author, to revise with care for the press. I am still of this opinion. I executed the task according to my best discretion. I do not pretend to infallibility of judgment; probably no two persons would decide alike in all cases of this kind, some of which involve minute distinctions of no great moment in themselves; nor am I sure that I should now in every instance approve my first decisions; but I feel that I have a right to claim the credit of integrity of purpose, and of having faithfully discharged the duty set before me, in strict conformity with the principles explained at large to the public in the Introduction to the first volume that was published.

But the heaviest charge is that of making *additions.* This charge is entirely without foundation. Knowing that not a single line, or fragment of a line, was intentionally *added* to the original text, throughout the whole twelve volumes of the work, I confess it was with no little surprise that I saw a passage quoted from a letter to Joseph Reed, as printed in "Washington's Writings," and declared by the writer in the Evening Post to be an invention of my own, the same not being found in what was supposed to be an exact copy of the original, printed in the "Life and Correspondence of Joseph Reed." The following is the quotation.

"The drift and design are obvious; *but is it possible that any sensible nation upon earth can be imposed upon by such a cobweb scheme or gauze covering?* But enough."

In his comment on this passage the writer says; "I assure you that the credit of all the rhetoric, all the invective, all the fancy, all the logic, and all the science of the lines here given in italics, belongs exclusively to Mr. Sparks, and when he imputed them to General Washington he robbed himself, and, perhaps you will think, the General also." Notwithstanding the writer's assurance, the quotation in italics, word for word as here printed, is in the original letter written by Washington. It was doubtless omitted in the "Life of Reed," by an oversight of the transcriber, or by some other accident. Every one knows how frequently accidents of this kind occur in the passing of manuscripts through a transcriber's and printer's hands; and the probability of errors from this source should teach caution to a critic, who has not positive evidence of his accuracy. The charge was certainly a grave one, and should not have been lightly uttered. It could not fail to excite suspicion and distrust. If an editor would allow himself to make an addition to the text in one place, he might do it in another, and in many others. No rules of editorial supervision could justify such a proceeding. I must repeat, therefore, that not a line has been anywhere intentionally or knowingly *added* to the text, as contained either in the letter-books or the originals from which the letters were copied for the press.

In the recent article mentioned above, Lord Mahon is quoted as saying; "Mr. Sparks has printed no part of the correspondence precisely as Washington wrote it, but has greatly altered, and, as he thinks, corrected and embellished it." So loose and sweeping a charge needs only be met by a plain denial of its truth, and a rebuke for its rashness. How could Lord Mahon affirm, that "no part" is printed as written, unless he had read the whole work, and compared each letter with the original? Has he ever made this comparison? Certainly not, because he has never seen the originals at all; and there is no proof that he has compared a fiftieth, or even a hundredth part, with other printed copies where they exist. His Lordship also undertakes to inform his readers what the editor "thinks"; but I assure him that the editor never had such a thought, nor ever dreamed of embellishing Washington's language in any manner whatever, nor of correcting it, except for the press, as above described.

As to the general execution of the work, I certainly had the best reason to believe, at the time of its publication, and afterwards, that my labors were satisfactory to the public, and merited praise, but I shall again recur to this point. Meantime I may, perhaps, be excused for inserting two letters, bearing upon it, from Chief Justice Marshall.

"Richmond, May 6th, 1834.

"Dear Sir; Mr. Thompson has forwarded to me the second and third volumes of the Writings of Washington, for which I am greatly indebted to you. I have perused them with much gratification. The work is greatly enriched by the additions, which your careful researches have enabled you to make to the papers you obtained at Mount Vernon. Your notes of illustration are extremely valuable. But I have read no part of these volumes with so much pleasure, as the series of maxims under the head of 'Rules of Civility and Decent Behavior in Company and Conversation.' These rules, of which I had never before heard, furnish a key with which to open the original character of this truly great man.

"With great and respectful esteem,

"I am your obedient

"J. MARSHALL."

After receiving three more volumes, Judge Marshall wrote again as follows.

"RICHMOND, April 29th, 1835.

"Dear Sir; I have deferred acknowledging the receipt of your favor of the 4th, until I should have it in my power to look over three additional volumes of your great work, which you have had the kindness to forward to me through Mr. Sanxay. I am much indebted to you for this continued and gratifying attention.

"Our Washington appears himself, and consequently to advantage, in the full-length portrait you have given of him. Your illustrative notes are very interesting, and add much, in my opinion, to the value of the text. That in the Appendix to the fifth volume, which develops Conway's Cabal, is peculiarly so. Many of the letters had not previously been seen by the public.

"The papers in the Appendix to the sixth volume, which show the difference of opinion between the King and Lord

North respecting the American war, disclose an historical fact which was entirely unknown, at least in this country. The obstinacy with which his Majesty pursued his original plan, though previously pretty well understood, is presented in a still stronger light than I had imagined. The more rational views entertained by Lord North were not even suspected.

"The fact to which you allude, as to Champe, had been noticed by me when originally perusing the letters. I think it not improbable that the thing might have been in contemplation before the execution of André, and that the hope of saving him was at first mixed with that of punishing Arnold. That the first object had become unattainable, was probably forgotten when the narrative was composed.

"I wish you all the fame and success to which your well-directed and laudable researches entitle you, and am, dear sir, with great respect and esteem,

"Your obliged and obedient

"J. Marshall."

These letters were written by a man, who, from his intimate knowledge of Washington's papers, after having had the originals in his possession for several years, and studied them minutely, was more competent than any other person to form a correct judgment of the manner in which they had been edited. He had examined and approved the general plan proposed for the work before it was begun, and here is an unqualified approval of the details of its execution, after the first half was completed.

## LETTER II.

### THE PRINCIPLES AND RULES ADOPTED IN EDITING THE WORK.

When a man is censured for his acts or opinions, the reasons and grounds on which they rest, especially if he has frankly and fully disclosed them, ought, in all fairness, to be made known at the same time. How else can an impartial judgment be formed, or the real merits of a case be understood? These dictates of justice and candor were overlooked by the writer in the Evening Post, as well as by Lord Mahon, who seems to have followed closely in his steps. No intimation is given, that the editor of "Washington's Writings" had explained with precision and fulness the plan of the work, and the principles by which his editorial labors were to be directed, and that he had carefully adhered to this plan and these principles.

Readers kept in ignorance of these facts might easily be led by the writer's charges and invectives to entertain the suspicion, that the editor had practised a deception upon the public, or at least had taken liberties which were designed to be concealed. As nothing can be further from the truth, such a suspicion should have been prevented by the more candid course of presenting the subject in its complete aspect and just relations.

The following passage, illustrative of these remarks, and not even alluded to by the writer in his strictures, is taken from the Introduction to the volume of "Washington's Writings" that was first published, being the second in the series.

"It has been a task of some difficulty to determine what general principles should be adopted, in selecting the parts for publication from the whole body of papers left by Washington. In the first place, the mass of manuscripts, which extends to eighty volumes, consisting chiefly of letters, is so large as to preclude the idea of publishing more than a comparatively small portion. Again, from the nature of the correspondence, being mostly official, and many of the letters having been written to different persons on the same subject, there are necessarily frequent repetitions, and numerous particulars constantly intervening, which, though essential at the time in the transactions to which they relate, have no longer any interest or moment. Of this description are the innumerable details incident to the subordinate arrangements of an army, such as supplies, provisions, clothing, camp equipage, arms, ammunition, and other points of minor consideration, which engaged the incessant care of the Commander-in-chief, and entered largely into his correspondence even with Congress, and the highest officers, both civil and military. To print all the materials of this kind would not only be useless in itself, but would add so much to the size and expense of the work, as at the same time to make it cumbersome and unattractive to readers, and raise its cost above the means of many individuals, who may wish to possess these personal records and authentic memorials of the acts, opinions, and character of the Father of his Country.

"Under these circumstances, I have endeavored to pursue such a course as would the most effectually attain the object to be desired, in bringing these papers before the public; namely, to exhibit the writings of Washington in a manner that will render strict justice to the imperishable name of their author, and contribute the greatest advantage to his countrymen, both at the present time and in future ages. For this purpose I have laid down two rules, which I have labored to follow with as much discrimination as possible; first, to select such parts as have a permanent value, on account of the historical facts which they contain, whether in relation to actual events, or to the political designs and operations in which Washington was a leading or conspicuous agent; secondly, to comprise such other parts as contain the views, opinions, counsels, and reflections of the writer on all kinds of topics, showing thereby the structure of his mind, its powers and resources, and the strong and varied points of his character. Upon this plan, it has been my study to go carefully through the manuscripts, without regard to what has heretofore been made public, and gather from the whole, and combine into one body, the portions most important for their intrinsic value and historical characteristics; so that the work, in its complete form, may be a depository of all the writings of Washington which it is essential to preserve, either as illustrating his political and private life, or the history of his country during the long and brilliant period of his public career.

"According to this plan, when a letter throughout bears the features above described, it will be printed entire, as will, in every case, the addresses, speeches, messages, circulars, and other state papers, issued by him from time to time. But many of the letters, both in the public and private correspondence, for the reasons already assigned, will necessarily be printed with omissions of unimportant passages, relating chiefly to topics or facts evanescent in their nature, and temporary in their design. Special care will be taken, nevertheless, in all such omissions, that the sense shall not be marred, nor the meaning of the writer in any manner perverted or obscured. Nor is this difficult, because the omitted passages usually treat upon separate and distinct subjects, and may be removed without injury to the remaining portions of the letter.

"It ought to be premised here, that, in preparing the manuscripts for the press, I have been obliged sometimes to use a latitude of discretion, rendered unavoidable by the mode in which the papers have been preserved. They are uniformly copied into volumes, and this task appears to have been performed, except in the Revolutionary correspondence, by incompetent or very careless transcribers. Gross blunders constantly occur, which not unfrequently destroy the sense, and which never could have existed in the original drafts. In these cases I have, of course, considered it a duty, appertaining to the functions of a faithful editor, to hazard such corrections as the construction of the sentence manifestly warranted, or a cool judgment dictated. On some occasions, the writer himself, through haste or inadvertence, may have fallen into an awkward use of words, faults of grammar, or inaccuracies of style, and when such occur from this source, I have equally felt bound to correct them. It would be an act of unpardonable injustice to any author, after his death, to bring forth compositions, and particularly letters, written with no design to their publication, and commit them to the press without previously subjecting them to a careful revision. This exercise of an editor's duty, however, I have thought it allowable to extend only to verbal and grammatical mistakes or inaccuracies, maintaining a scrupulous caution that the author's meaning and purpose should thereby in no degree be changed or affected."

These statements embrace the whole ground, and they are so full and clear, so free from disguise and ambiguity, so direct and explicit in their details, that I cannot now perceive, upon a careful revision, how any reader could misapprehend their meaning. They went out to the world with the first specimen of the work, and, during its progress of four years through the press, no critic, friendly or hostile, no individual, within my knowledge, ever hinted that the plan, or the rules for executing it, were founded on erroneous principles, or were perverted in their application. If objections had been offered from any quarter in a candid spirit, accompanied by adequate reasons, they would have led me to reconsider the subject, and perhaps to modify the plan; for it must be evident, that I could have no other motive than that of executing the work in such a manner as would be approved by an enlightened public opinion. This approval was expressed in numerous instances, and without any censorious comments or qualifying suggestions, that have come to my knowledge.

In regard to omissions, it must be recollected that the whole work is only a selection, and purports to be nothing more. This is abundantly explained in the above extract from the Introduction. I am certainly safe in saying, that more than two thirds of the whole collection of manuscripts were necessarily omitted, in consequence of the limited extent to which it was proposed to carry the work.

Lord Mahon has discovered a passage in Marshall's Life of Washington, which he takes pains to inform his readers is not found in the "Writings." How was it possible to compress matter sufficient for thirty or forty volumes into twelve, without omissions? Or what improper motive can be imagined to have influenced the editor in omitting the particular passage remarked by Lord Mahon?

To decide what papers should be selected in preference to others, where nearly all of them were in a certain degree important and valuable, was felt to be a responsible, delicate, and difficult task, requiring a discriminating judgment, and perfect impartiality, in estimating their contents. Moreover, it was precisely one of those cases in which any two minds, acting under different impressions, though aiming at the same end, would be likely often to differ? Under these circumstances the course was taken which was believed to be the best suited to guard against erroneous decisions and estimates. The whole collection of papers, including as well the letters written by Washington as those received by him, was first perused deliberately and with careful attention.

This was the labor of nearly a year. The letters chosen during this perusal were transcribed, and they formed a mass much too large for the intended work. This mass was several times revised, and was reduced to a smaller compass, with constant reference to the letter-books for the purpose of comparison and of substituting other letters, which, upon further examination, might seem to have higher claims, either as preserving a more connected series of historical events, or as showing in a stronger light the opinions, intellectual traits, and personal characteristics of the author. In this way the selection for the whole work was made; and whatever faults of judgment may appear as to the choice of one letter instead of another, I can truly affirm that the task was not performed with negligence or haste, nor without due consideration of every case as it arose. The selection was reduced by M. Guizot to six volumes in the French edition; Von Raumer comprised the German edition in two volumes; and a London editor thought the same number sufficient for the British public.

The propriety of omitting parts of letters, and retaining other parts, may, perhaps, at first view, be thought questionable. But when it is considered that parts of letters, treating upon totally distinct and unconnected topics, are in reality the same as so many distinct letters, it is obvious that to omit such parts differs in no respect from omitting separate letters. Moreover, if entire letters had in every instance been printed, it would have been necessary to leave out of the work much that was valuable and important, which is now included, and frequently to repeat the same matter, and sometimes in the same language.

In the correspondence during the Revolution, it often happened that several letters were written nearly at the same time to different persons, the President of Congress, the governors of States, officers of the army, or other official characters, in which not only the same facts were communicated, and the same topics discussed, but whole paragraphs were almost literally transcribed from one letter into others. These repetitions grew out of the nature of the business in hand, and could not have been avoided without unnecessary circumlocutions and strained attempts to seek a variety of language for expressing the same ideas. As to letters of this description, it was the practice to print some one of them entire, and to select from the others such parts as were free from repetitions. But in all omissions, whether for these reasons or others, whether short or long, special care was taken not to break off in the midst of a topic or train of thought, and not, by any abrupt transition, to weaken or obscure the sense of the author.

By these principles and rules I was guided in selecting the papers for the press. That the work is faultless in this part of its execution, or in any other, I cannot suppose, being fully aware of the innumerable chances of error in every undertaking so extensive and complex. Letters may possibly have been omitted through oversight, or a mistake of judgment, or by accident, which might be advantageously substituted for some of those retained. It would be strange if it were not so. But it was never imagined that a letter would be lost to the world because it was not comprised in this selection. It was presumed that such of the large mass of papers, still unprinted, as have any interest for the public, would be brought out at some future time. By the contract between Judge Washington and Chief Justice Marshall on the one part, and myself on the other, the copyright of the work belonged, in equal shares, to them and to me; and the rights thus secured to them are now held by their heirs. The Washington manuscripts were purchased by Congress, several years after this contract was made, and with a full understanding of its terms and conditions. All the papers not covered by this copyright are as free to be published now, as any others in the possession of the government.

## LETTER III.

### THE CONDITION IN WHICH MANY OF WASHINGTON'S LETTERS WERE LEFT IN REGARD TO THE TEXT.

In this letter it is proposed to speak further of the *text* of "Washington's Writings," as found in his letter-books and in the originals sent to his correspondents. The following extract from the Preface to the work bears directly on this point.

"In regard to the text, also, it is proper here to repeat what has been said in another place, that frequent embarrassments have occurred. It was Washington's custom, in all his letters of importance, first to write drafts, which he transcribed. In making the transcripts he sometimes deviated from the drafts, omitting, inserting, and altering parts of sentences; nor did he always correct the drafts, so as to make them accord with the letters as sent to his correspondents. These imperfect drafts were laid aside, and from time to time copied by an amanuensis into the letter-books. Hence the drafts, as now recorded, do not in all cases agree precisely with the originals that were sent away. My researches have brought under my inspection many of these original letters. Regarding them as containing the genuine text, I have preferred it to that in the letter-books, and it has accordingly been adopted wherever it could be done.

"But the discrepancies are of little moment, relating to the style, and not to the substance. For the most part, I have been obliged to rely on the letter-books; and, for the reasons here mentioned, it is probable that the printed text may not in every particular be the same as in the originals, that is, the corrected copies, which were sent to his correspondents. These remarks apply chiefly to private letters, written when Washington was at Mount Vernon, and to those written during the French war. In the periods of the Revolution and the Presidency, much more exactness was observed; and, as far as my observation has extended, there is generally a literal accordance between the original letters and the transcripts in the letter-books."

These remarks were intended distinctly to explain the actual state of the case, and the embarrassments attending it, with the view both of conveying proper information to the public, and of removing every ground of suspicion and misapprehension in regard to the manner in which these embarrassments were met by the editor.

As an illustration of the above statement, and as an evidence of the facility with which hasty criticism may deceive itself and run to false conclusions, we may recur to a prominent passage selected by the writer in the Evening Post, in support of his charge of alteration and perversion of the text. He quotes the following extract from one of Washington's letters, as printed in the "Life of Joseph Reed," dated December 12th, 1778.

"What did or could prompt the knight (Sir Henry Clinton) to this expedition, *is beyond the reach of my conception*, considering the unseasonableness of it. Three things only appeared to me probable; a rescue of the Convention troops, a stroke at the rear of our army, or a surprise of *the* posts in the Highlands. The two first I had seen perfectly out of his reach before I left the North River, and not conceiving that he could *miss it so much* in point of intelligence as to mistime matters so egregiously, (if either of the *other two* was his object,) it followed of consequence, that the last must be his aim; and though I had left him, as I thought, in a state of security, and in the hands of a good officer, McDougall, I could not help being uneasy, lest *some* disaster might *befall them*. I posted back from Elizabethtown on the morning of the 5th, and got within twelve or fifteen miles of King's Ferry, when I was met by an express informing me that the enemy had landed at that place, *set fire to two small log'd houses*, *destroyed* nine barrels of *spoiled* herrings and had *set sail* for New York."

In contrast with this passage, the writer produces the following, as printed in "Washington's Writings."

"What did or could prompt the knight to this expedition, *I am at a loss to discover*, considering the unseasonableness of it. Three things only appear to me probable; a rescue of the Convention troops, a stroke at the rear of our army, or a surprise of *our* posts in the Highlands. The two first I had seen perfectly out of his reach before I left the North River; and, not conceiving that he could *be so much out* in point of intelligence, as to mistime matters so egregiously, if either of the *two first* was his object, it followed, of consequence, that the last must be his aim; and, though I had left them, as I thought, in a state of security, and in the hands of a good officer, McDougall, I could not help being uneasy lest *a* disaster might *happen; and* I posted back from Elizabethtown *at four o'clock* in the morning of the 5th, and got within twelve or fifteen miles of King's Ferry, when I was met by an express, informing me that the enemy had landed at that place, *burned two or three log-houses*, with nine barrels of *spoilt* herrings, and had *reëmbarked and sailed* for New York *again*."

The editor is charged with having made all the alterations here indicated by the italics. To this charge no other reply is necessary, than that it is erroneous. The extract from the letter in "Washington's Writings" is printed exactly as it is recorded in the letter-book, from which it was transcribed for the press, except in two instances. Before *disaster* the letter *a* is inserted; the original text reads "lest disaster." In the letter-book are the words *logged houses*, (not *log'd* houses, as in Mr. Reed's copy,) and this was printed *log-houses*. Whether these corrections were made by me, or by the proof-reader, I cannot now undertake to determine. Nor am I bound to reconcile the discrepances between the two copies. I followed the only one in my possession.

Take another example from Marshall's "Life of Washington," (Vol. V. p. 15,) where is an extract from a letter to Governor Harrison, of Virginia, dated October 10th, 1784, and printed in the words following.

"I need not remark to you, Sir, that the flanks and rear of the United States are possessed by other powers, and formidable ones too; *nor need I press the necessity of applying* the cement of interest to bind all parts of the Union together by indissoluble bonds; especially *of binding* that part of it which lies immediately west of us, *to* the Middle States. For what ties, let me ask, should we have upon those people, how entirely unconnected with them shall we be, and what troubles may we not apprehend, if the Spaniards on their right, and Great Britain on their left, instead of throwing *impediments* in their way, as they now do, should hold out lures for their trade and alliance? When they get strength, which will be sooner than most people conceive, *what* will be the consequence of their having formed close *commercial* connections with both, or either of those powers? It needs not, in my opinion, the gift of prophecy to foretell."

In "Washington's Writings," this letter is printed from the letter-book, in which the above paragraph is word for word as follows.

"I need not remark to you, Sir, that the flanks and rear of the United States are possessed by other powers, and formidable ones too; *nor how necessary it is to apply* the cement of interest to bind all parts of the Union together by indissoluble bonds, especially that part of it, which lies immediately west of us, *with* the Middle States. For what ties, let me ask, should we have upon those people? How entirely unconnected with them shall we be, and what troubles may we not apprehend, if the Spaniards on their right, and Great Britain on their left, instead of throwing *stumbling-blocks* in their way, as they now do, should hold out lures for their trade and alliance? *What*, when they get strength, which will be sooner than most people conceive, (*from the emigration of foreigners, who will have no particular predilection towards us, as well as from the removal of our own citizens*,) will be the consequence of their having formed close connections with both or either of those powers, *in a commercial way?* It needs not, in my opinion, the gift of prophecy to foretell."

Here are what may be considered important variations. Whence do they arise? It would be difficult to ascertain; or to decide what text was adopted by Judge Marshall. I had no other than that in the letter-book.

We may draw another illustration from a letter to Richard Henry Lee, dated December 14th, 1784.

The following paragraph is taken from the original letter.

"Individual States opposing the measures of the United States, encroaching upon the territory of *one another*, and setting up old and obsolete claims, is verifying the predictions of our enemies, and *in reality* is truly unfortunate. If the western tribes are as well disposed to treat with us as the *northern Indians* have been, and will cede a competent district of *country* northwest of the Ohio to answer our present purposes, it *would* be a circumstance as unexpected as pleasing to me; for it was apprehended, *if they agreed to the latter at all, it would be reluctantly;* but the example of the *Six Nations*, who, if they have not relinquished their claim, have pretensions to a large part of those lands, may have a powerful influence on the western gentry, and smooth the way for the commissioners, who have proceeded to *Fort Pitt*."

The same paragraph transcribed from the letter-book is as follows.

"Individual States opposing the measures of the United States, encroaching upon the territory of *each other*, and setting up old and obsolete claims, is verifying the prediction of our enemies, and is truly unfortunate. If the western tribes are as well disposed to treat with us as the *Six Nations* have been, and will cede a competent district of *land* northwest of the Ohio to answer our present purposes, it *will* be a circumstance as unexpected as pleasing to me; for it was apprehended *that they would agree to the latter reluctantly, if at all;* but the example of the *northern*

*Indians*, who, if they have not relinquished their claim, have pretensions to a large part of those lands, may have a powerful influence on the western gentry, and smooth the way for the commissioners, who have proceeded to *Cuyahoga*."

These specimens will serve to show the state of the text in a large portion of Washington's letters, as they now exist in manuscript, particularly those written at Mount Vernon, and others of a private nature written elsewhere. The originals sent to his correspondents seldom agree throughout in phraseology with the copies retained on record. Moreover, these copies are constantly marred by the blunders or mistakes of illiterate or careless transcribers. For the most part, there was no resource for the editor but to follow the letter-books. Hence the text of many letters in "Washington's Writings," compared with other copies, whether found in print or in manuscript, must necessarily afford abundant materials for the kind of criticisms in which the writer in the Evening Post, and Lord Mahon, have indulged themselves with so much freedom of censure.

Another example, still more striking, may be mentioned. Washington kept a copy of his official correspondence during his military services in the last French war before the Revolution, written on sheets loosely stitched together. Some twenty or thirty years afterwards he revised this manuscript, making numerous erasures, interlineations, and corrections in almost every letter. This corrected copy was then transcribed into bound volumes under his own direction. Which is now the genuine text? Which would Washington himself have printed?

The one in the letter-books was adopted, because it seemed obvious, that, after the pains he had taken to prepare it, he intended that copy for permanent preservation and use. It would be easy to cavil here, and say that we have not the precise language employed by Washington to convey his thoughts at the time the letters were written, but a garbled substitute introduced at a much later day. Yet this was an act of his own, and certainly no editor would be justified in disregarding it. In these letters, therefore, the same kind of discrepancies will necessarily appear, as in the cases alluded to above, between the printed text and that of the originals sent out to his correspondents.

Before closing these remarks, I may perhaps be pardoned for adding a few other particulars respecting the execution of the work.

General Washington bequeathed all his papers and books to his nephew, Bushrod Washington, by whom they were retained at Mount Vernon. It is well known that Chief Justice Marshall had the free use of these papers while writing his "Life of Washington." For many years afterwards they were not consulted for any historical purpose, although some progress was made by Judge Washington in selecting a portion of them for the press. This design was abandoned, however, and, by a contract with those gentlemen, the task of carrying out a similar design on a larger scale than had been contemplated was assigned to me, under certain regulations and conditions agreed upon by the parties, and defined in the contract. Immediately after signing this contract in the city of Washington, I was engaged three months at Mount Vernon in a general inspection and arrangement of the papers, which were ultimately transferred to Boston. They remained in my possession ten years, till the publication of the work was completed.

It was an essential feature of the plan, that the work was not to be merely a compilation of Washington's letters, but was to comprise additional and illustrative matter gathered from various original sources, which would give a new value to the letters, and afford new developments of the private and historical character of the author. Fully aware of the importance of being prepared to execute the work thoroughly and faithfully, according to the plan proposed, by previous research and study, I visited the public offices of all the old Thirteen States, and personally inspected the papers in them relating to the Revolution, and particularly such as would illustrate Washington's letters, and the events with which he was more or less connected. Copies of the most valuable of these papers, constituting a rich collection of historical materials, were obtained. With the same object in view, and with similar results, I sought out and examined the private papers, then remaining, of many of the chief actors in the Revolution.

Having thus procured such aids as my opportunities would permit in this country, I then made a voyage to Europe for the express purpose of continuing my researches there. I passed a year in the public offices of London and Paris, diligently employed in examining the voluminous collections of papers contained in them relating to the American war, and treating both of political and military affairs. By the courtesy and liberality of the governments of Great Britain and France, I was allowed to have free access to these papers, and to procure copies of such as were suited to my object.

These facts are briefly stated, to show that the work was not undertaken with a narrow estimate of its importance; that neither time, nor labor, nor expense was spared in the preparation; and that in these respects the editor cannot be charged with haste or negligence. The original materials thus collected from many sources, and possessing the highest degree of authenticity, furnished the notes and appendices to the several volumes. Good judges have not failed to see in them a large body of interesting facts, which had not before been made public, and which contribute to elucidate at once the character and deeds of Washington, and that portion of the history of the country with which these are so intimately blended. It was my steady aim throughout, while enlarging the bounds of historical knowledge, to elicit truth as far as it could be done by bringing together contemporary testimonies of unquestionable authority, and thus to render justice to the designs, conduct, and character of the principal actors, to whatever side or party they might belong.

The contest between England and her former colonies partook of many of the characteristics of a civil war, inflaming the passions and perverting the judgment of both parties; and it was a necessary consequence, that there should be erroneous opinions and false impressions in this country concerning the motives, policy, and plans of the British ministry, as well as of their military officers commanding in America, and that these should give a coloring to the correspondence of the time.

In cases of this kind, special care was taken, when practicable, to correct such errors, as well as others derived from a defective knowledge of facts, by a free use of the materials procured from the British offices, in which the ministers and the military commanders speak for themselves. A British historian might perhaps find something to commend in the results of these attempts, which were at least prompted by a high motive; and I am persuaded that every American reader will be pleased to see the name of Washington associated with any historical illustrations tending to establish truth and justice.

www.ingramcontent.com/pod-product-compliance
Lightning Source LLC
LaVergne TN
LVHW011124110826
845150LV00008B/2241

* 9 7 8 1 4 1 8 1 9 5 2 1 2 *